BADEN-POWELL
Founder of the Boy Scouts

Allan Stewart
-1900

BADEN-POWELL
Founder of the Boy Scouts

By Pauline York Brower

CHILDRENS PRESS®
CHICAGO

**Dedication:
To my grandson
Benjamin York Jones**

*The author wishes to acknowledge with thanks the assistance of Grant Mitzell,
Boy Scout of America, and William Gold, retired Boy Scout of America volunteer
and professional, in preparation of this manuscript.*

Library of Congress Cataloging-in-Publication Data

Brower, Pauline.
    Baden-Powell : founder of the Boy Scouts / by Pauline
York Brower.
    p.   cm. — (Picture story biographies)
    Summary: Examines the lifetime achievements of the
man who founded the Boy Scout Movement in Great
Britain and saw it expand all over the world.
    ISBN 0-516-04173-8
    1.   Baden-Powell of Gilwell, Robert Stephenson Smyth
Baden-Powell, Baron, 1857-1941 — Juvenile literature.
2.   Boy Scouts — Great Britain — Biography — Juvenile
literature.   [1.   Baden-Powell of Gilwell, Robert
Stephenson Smyth Baden-Powell, Baron, 1857-1941.
2.   Boy Scouts — Great Britain.]   I. Title.   II. Series.
HS3268.2.B33B76   1989
369.43'092 — dc20   89-33750
[B]   CIP
[92]   AC

Photo Credits

Boy Scouts of America — Cover, 3, 4, 5, 6, 8,
9, 10, 12, 13 (2 photos), 15, 16 (right), 19,
22, 23, 24, 25 (2 photos), 27 (2 photos), 28,
29, 30, 31, 32
The Granger Collection — 1, 2, 7 (2 photos),
16 (left), 17 (2 photos), 20

"We, the Scouts of the World,
salute you, Sir Robert Baden-
Powell—Chief Scout of the World!"
A single voice, from hundreds of
Boy Scouts, called out this salute.

Baden-Powell, founder of the Boy
Scouts, was pleased and surprised.
Honoring him with this title, Chief
Scout of the World, was the final
event of the first Boy Scout Jamboree.

Boy Scouts from twenty-three
countries gathered in London,
England, for their first international
meeting in 1920. The Jamboree

lasted eight days. Scouts competed in tests and skills. They played games and ran races. They built bridges. The Scouts of many nations displayed skills in crafts and endurance.

The Jamboree brought back memories from Baden-Powell's past. He was one of seven children. His father took great pride in teaching his children about outdoor life and the secrets of nature.

Baden-Powell was born on February 22, 1857, in Oxford, England. He was given three names,

Four-year-old Stephe

The Granger Collection, New York
The Reverend Professor Baden-Powell

The Granger Collection, New York
Henrietta Grace Powell and her daughter Alice

Robert Stephenson Smyth Baden-Powell. His family called him Stephe. He had five brothers and a sister. His father was a professor at Oxford University.

When Stephe was three years old his father died. His mother, Henrietta Grace, raised her children as their father had wanted. She taught her young children to read and write. She also taught them the values of honor, duty, and self-reliance.

Stephe's older brothers took him camping and exploring. They taught him about plants and animals. He learned to make campfires. When the older brothers were away at boarding school, Stephe taught his younger brother and sister.

Young Stephe was a small boy with curly red hair and freckles. He was full of energy. Studying nature and exploring in the woods were Stephe's favorite pastimes. During

Seven-year-old Stephe (top) with Warington and Frank (center) and Agnes and Baden, his younger sister and brother

Seventeen-year-old
Stephe attended
Charterhouse School.

bad weather Stephe kept busy
drawing and painting. He wrote
plays and acted in them.

Mrs. Baden-Powell arranged a
scholarship for Stephe. He enrolled
at Charterhouse School in London
when he was eleven. Stephe enjoyed
the school. He was interested in
most social activities, but he was not
a scholar. His teachers knew he was
bright. They also knew he was not
interested in schoolwork.

Stephe played the violin and the

Stephe (third from left) was on the Wimbledon rifle team in 1874.

flügelhorn. When the cadet corps needed a bugler, Stephe took the job. He wrote stories for the school magazine, acted in plays, and sang in the choir. When the curtain went up, Stephe was there. He liked to make people laugh. He was a performer.

Charterhouse School was surrounded by woods. Stephe enjoyed hiking by himself. He pretended to be a trapper or an Indian scout. He learned the habits of the animals and birds. One time he trapped a rabbit, cleaned it, and cooked it over a smokeless fire. Later in his life he said the adventures in the woods gave him "health of body and mind."

Holidays from school were busy. Stephe and his older brothers took boating and camping trips. They sailed the rivers and seaports of

England. These outings were Stephe's real school.

During his last year at Charterhouse, the Baden-Powell family planned Stephe's future. His interests in acting and art were never considered in the plan. The family decided he should take the entrance exams for Oxford University.

Stephe's family was shocked when they received the exam results. Stephe had failed! Stephe felt like an outcast. His older brothers had earned honors at Oxford. He had let his family down.

Stephe learned that agents from Her Majesty's Army were holding exams to find qualified young officers. His grandfather had been an admiral. His uncle was an officer in the army. Stephe had doubts, but he decided to take the exams. He spent hours studying subjects he had

not learned in school. The exams took twelve days.

Days later a family friend gave Stephe the newspaper with exam results. Seven hundred and eighteen young men took the exams. Stephe had placed second for the army cavalry! What a happy celebration for the Baden-Powell family.

On September 11, 1876, Stephe became Sublieutenant Baden-Powell. A few weeks later he sailed from Portsmouth Harbor to India. This was the beginning of a long adventure and a new life. With his new life came a new name. Stephe was now Baden-Powell, nicknamed B-P by his friends.

Baden-Powell's drawing of the oxcart that carried him to his military post in India. B-P became a captain when he was twenty-six.

Baden-Powell's army career lasted over thirty years. He served most of his career in India and Africa. His work was rewarded with promotions, awards, honors and medals for outstanding achievement. The men serving under B-P considered him a fair and firm leader. His commanding officers recognized his special talents.

Baden-Powell was an army scout and an intelligence officer. As a scout he went ahead of the troops and explored the land. He observed the movement of the enemy and made drawings of the action. At one time he drew maps of a six-hundred-mile area for his commanding officer.

Baden-Powell trained British and native troops. B-P was surprised that so few soldiers knew the skills of scouting. He wrote a handbook on scouting for his men. He taught them to imagine what the enemy was thinking and planning.

Troop morale was important to B-P. He organized plays to entertain the men. When there were no battles to fight, B-P wrote articles and books. He drew sketches of battle areas in India and Africa. His articles and drawings were published in London newspapers.

B-P
sketched
battle
scenes.

The most famous battle of Baden-Powell's army career took place in South Africa during the Boer War. This was a war between England and the colonists of South Africa. B-P and his men were defending the town of Mafeking. They were surrounded by the enemy Boers. The defenders of Mafeking had very few cannons and guns. B-P used his quick wits and imagination to "bluff with boldness."

B-P had his men make fake mines. They planted them around the town as the enemy Boers watched from a distance. Baden-Powell made one real mine of dynamite. His men exploded this mine as everyone watched. The enemy believed the fake mines were real.

Then Baden-Powell had his men put the old cannons on railroad cars.

Mrs. Davies (left) was just one of the women who fought in the trenches. The Mafeking officers were: Standing: Major Panzera, Captain Ryan, Captain Greener, Major Lord Edward Cecil, Captain Gordon Wilson, Captain Hanbury-Tracey, Captain Cowan. Seated: Major Godley, Major Vyvyan, Magistrate Bell, Colonel B-P, Major Whiteley, Colonel Hore, Dr. Hayes. On the ground: Lieutenant Moncrieffe.

When B-P thought the Boers were ready to attack, he ran the railroad cars around the tracks with cannons blazing. The surprised Boers were so amazed they retreated.

As the months passed, the townspeople of Mafeking built bomb shelters and rationed food. They ate soup made from food for animals. B-P planned projects and entertainment to boost their morale. At times he thought of surrendering.

Colonel Baden-Powell issued special money during the siege.

B-P stands atop his bomb shelter

After two hundred and seventeen days, the British Army Relief Force reached Mafeking. Baden-Powell was taken by surprise when he saw that the relief officer was his younger brother.

During the long siege, news of Mafeking leaked through enemy lines. London papers often ran stories of Mafeking's struggle to survive. English people prayed for the defenders of Mafeking.

When news reached London that relief forces were in Mafeking, crowds gathered to sing and cheer. Newspaper headlines declared Colonel Baden-Powell the savior of Mafeking. Queen Victoria sent her congratulations. The war office promoted Baden-Powell to Major General. He was the nation's hero!

As the "Hero of Mafeking" B-P

Hundreds of people celebrated the British victory at Mafeking.

received hundreds of letters from boys and girls. People wrote him asking for advice. He answered every letter, amazed at his popularity. He didn't feel like a hero.

His latest book, *Aids To Scouting*, had recently been published. Baden-Powell was pleased to learn the book was selling well. Other countries used the book to train their soldiers.

Parades were held honoring Baden-Powell, the "Hero of Mafeking."

Becoming "Hero of Mafeking" changed Baden-Powell's life. Early in 1903 he was appointed Inspector General of the British Cavalry. While inspecting the cavalry in Scotland, B-P agreed to review a Boys Brigade drill. The founder of the organization, William Smith, drilled his boys like little soldiers. They wore uniforms and carried toy guns. Thousands watched as the boys marched past the "Hero of Mafeking."

Baden-Powell congratulated the boys. He suggested to William Smith that a variety of activities would attract more boys to the brigade. William Smith challenged B-P to write a program on scouting for boys.

Drilling boys like soldiers did not impress Baden-Powell. He thought the program for boys should develop their sense of adventure and offer them many more experiences. B-P believed that "drills in observation would sharpen the wits of the boys."

William Smith's challenge to write a program for boys stayed in Baden-Powell's mind. Two years later, B-P put his plan on paper. He titled his program "Scouting for Boys." B-P provided lessons in using a compass.

''Fire lighting with two matches only'' was a skill B-P introduced. He stressed hiking, camping, and tracking as character builders. He outlined first aid techniques.

Baden-Powell had reviewed several boys' organizations. Two of the groups, the Woodcraft Indians and the Sons of Daniel Boone, were from America.

Baden-Powell's plan for boys was different from those he had

The camp was
a tremendous
success.

observed. He decided to test his
ideas. In 1907 he selected twenty-
one boys for a two-week camping
trip. The boys camped at Brownsea
Island in England. The camp was a
great success. Baden-Powell's
interest and enthusiasm increased.

All of his notes and thoughts
came together. By 1908 he had
developed his outline plan into a
book titled *Scouting For Boys.*

His goal for Boy Scouts was to

develop good citizens. Baden-Powell outlined drills to build physical health and strong mental attitudes. He wanted the boys to have experiences with nature for spiritual growth. The Boy Scout Movement stressed teamwork and helping others. Chapters in his Scouting Manual included "Our Duties as Citizens," "Saving Life," and "Being Prepared."

Scouting for Boys and his ideas for

Baden-Powell at a Boy Scout Camp in 1908

this new organization were an instant success. General Baden-Powell pushed the Boy Scout Movement forward with great enthusiasm. He traveled the British Isles taking the plan for Boy Scouts to the people. Thousands of Boy Scout troops sprang up in the wake of his talks. Boys in broad-brimmed hats and bright colored scarves hiked the countrysides. Smoke from campfires filled the country air. The Boy Scout Movement grew so fast that B-P started a weekly paper, *The Scout*, to get news to the members.

Scouting for Boys was published In 1908. The book's cover was designed by John Hassall.

An executive committee for Boy Scouts held its first meeting in 1909. Keeping up with the growth of the Boy Scout Movement was their challenge. Hundreds of volunteer Scoutmasters caught B-P's excitement and joined the movement.

Baden-Powell made the difficult

B-P drew the first sketch of a Boy Scout uniform.

decision to take an early retirement. He had spent most of his life in the army. Now he would dedicate his life to the Boy Scout Movement.

The king of England knighted Baden-Powell for his heroism at Mafeking and his success as founder of Boy Scouts. After the ceremony the king suggested that Sir Robert Baden-Powell bring his Scouts to Windsor Castle for a royal review.

Scouting for Boys was translated into many languages. With no effort from Baden-Powell, volunteers in Belgium, France, Holland, Denmark, Sweden, and Russia taught scouting to their boys.

The Boy Scout Movement spread to other continents. By 1908 groups had organized in Canada, Australia, and New Zealand. Scouts met in India in 1909. In Chili, Brazil, and Argentina the Boy Scout program

took root. Scoutmasters started groups in the Orient. Early in 1910 the United States joined the Boy Scout Movement.

Two years after retiring from the army, Baden-Powell met and married Olave Soames. She traveled with B-P promoting the Boy Scout Movement around the world. Olave worked with B-P's sister Agnes to develop a program for girls called the Girl Guides. At about the same

time, Juliette Low, a good friend of
Baden-Powell's, organized the Girl
Scouts of America. B-P was a strong
supporter of both programs.

Groups for younger boys, called
Wolf Cubs, found a place in the Boy
Scout Movement. The Rovers,
young men in their late teens,
became active in advanced Scouting.
Handicapped boys joined the Scouts.
Special tasks were written for Scouts
in wheelchairs.

The widespread growth of

Scouting continued. Baden-Powell's endless energy took him to the four corners of the world. His dream of world harmony grew with each international Boy Scout Jamboree.

The king of England honored Baden-Powell with a new title, Lord Baden-Powell of Gilwell. The ceremony took place a few months before the third Jamboree.

Forty-two countries and fifteen thousand boys attended the 1929 Jamboree. The Scouts of the world now numbered two million.

Baden-Powell attended his last Jamboree in 1937. His health was failing and he knew the meeting was his last. At the international meeting in Holland he stood beside Queen Wilhelmina. Together they watched thousands of boys march behind the flags of their nations. Shortly before Baden-Powell spoke to the group, a thundering chant filled the air: "B-P—B-P—B-P—B-P—B-P."

Baden-Powell's emotional response was, "The time has come for me to say good-bye. You know that many of us will never meet again in this world. I am in my eighty-first year and am nearing the end of my life. Most of you are in the beginning and I want your lives to be happy and successful. You can make them so by doing your best to carry out the Scout Law all your days, whatever your station and wherever you are.''

B-P was satisfied in knowing that Scouting had enriched the lives of millions of boys. Lord Baden-Powell knew the Boy Scouts were making a better world.

On January 8, 1941, the Chief Scout of the World died at his home in Kenya, Africa.

Boy Scouts from around the world attended the funeral of Baden-Powell.

BADEN-POWELL
Founder of the Boy Scouts

1857	February 22, Robert Stephenson Smyth Baden-Powell, born in Oxford, England
1868-76	Attended Charterhouse School, London
1876	Joined the British Army, commissioned a Sublieutenant
1877	Promoted to Lieutenant while serving in India
1883	Promoted to Captain at age 26
1887	Became aide-de-camp to General Henry Smyth, South Africa
1890	Promoted to Brevet Major
1890-93	Served in Malta as intelligence officer
1896	Promoted to Brevet Lieutenant Colonel, awarded Ashanti campaign medal
1897	Commander of the 5th Dragoon Guards in India, taught scouting to cavalrymen
1899	Boer War, Mafeking
1903	Hero of the Boer War, promoted to Lieutenant General
1903	Established South African Constabulary
1903	Inspector General of Cavalry, England
1907	Held two-week camping trip on Brownsea Island
1908	Knight Commander of the Victorian Order
1909	First Boy Scout Executive Committee meeting
1910	Retired from army to work with Boy Scout Movement
1912	Married Olave Soames
1916	Organized Wolf Cubs in England
1920	First Boy Scout Jamboree, England
1924	Second Boy Scout Jamboree, Denmark
1929	Titled, Lord Baden-Powell of Gilwell
1929	Third Boy Scout Jamboree, England
1932	Fourth Boy Scout Jamboree, Hungary
1937	Fifth World Jamboree, Holland
1937	Scouts honored by King George VI
1937	Awarded the Order of Merit by King George VI
1937	Awarded Wateler Peace Prize for service to world peace
1941	January 8, Baden-Powell died in Kenya, Africa

BOOKS BY BADEN-POWELL

1884	*Reconnaissance and Scouting*
1885	*Cavalry Instruction*
1899	*Aids to Scouting for N.C.O.s and Men*
1908	*Scouting for Boys*
1909	*Yarns for Boy Scouts*
1910	*Scouting Games*
1912	*Handbook for Girl Guides*
1913	*Boy Scouts Beyond the Seas*
1916	*Young Knights of the Empire*
1918	*Girl Guiding*
1921	*What Scouts Can Do*
1922	*Roving to Success*
1927	*Life's Snags and How to Meet Them*
1935	*Scouting Round the World*
1936	*Adventuring to Manhood*

INDEX

ABOUT THE AUTHOR

Pauline Brower attended the University of Southern California and the University of California at Los Angeles. Mrs. Brower was an associate editor of the Northern Virginia Newspapers, specializing in articles on colonial America. She co-authored the Living Heritage series for children with June Behrens. Her interest in writing for children led to scriptwriting for deaf children on local cable television. She wrote and produced an award-winning television series for New Jersey cable. Mrs. Brower has lectured in elementary schools on living history and writing. She is a former Girl Scout and looks forward to participating in her grandson's Cub Scout experiences. Pauline Brower lives with her husband in Corona Del Mar, California.